EMBRACE YOUR SHADOW

EMBRACE
YOUR
SHADOW

Audrey G. Adams

Divine Purpose Book Publishing

Valdosta, Georgia

EMBRACE YOUR SHADOW

Published by
Divine Purpose Book Publishing
Valdosta, Georgia
audrey.adams528@gmail.com

Audrey G. Adams, Publisher / Editorial Director
Yvonne Rose/Quality Press.info, Book Packager

DISCLAIMER

This content reflects the personal opinions of the author gathered from countless news articles, seminars, class notes, digital resources, speeches, lecture notes, and lived experiences and discussions. It is accurate and true to the best of her knowledge and should not be substituted for fact or advice in legal, political, or personal matters.

Dedication

I will begin by shouting, "What an AWESOME God we serve!" God works in mysterious ways. This past year of my life has been a challenging one, but with God and some isolation time I have been able to overcome the obstacles that took me to my knees. So, this dedication is an extra special one for me. This devotion is to a beautiful soul who God blessed me with almost two decades ago. This young woman has been with me during every moment of her life. To be a parent is not a right; it is a privilege, and I have cherished every single moment that I have spent with her over the years. No one could ever interfere with the powerful bond that we share.

The beautiful, smart, and mature young woman I dedicate this book to is my daughter, my best friend, Kamiila Jade. I love you with my whole heart and thank God for you every day. I pray that you continue to walk in the direction that God has assigned for you and that you always take what I have instilled in you to do wonderful successful things in life. You are talented and you are a beautiful soul who deserves the best in life. Remember, your destiny is for you and no one else. Whenever you may feel down or are questioning life's obstacles, remember that God gives a challenge to promote growth. I love you and wish you a life filled with countless smiles, success, and the abundance the Lord has promised you.

Acknowledgements

I want to thank God - my Healer, my Protector, my Strength, my Motivator, and my Redeemer - for giving me the gift of writing. This beautiful gift, which God has blessed me with enables me to inspire others and be a source of help during their seasons of depression, low self-esteem, relationship toxicity, and narcissistic abuse. I am beyond grateful that I can help those who need it most.

I also want to express a huge amount of love and gratitude to ALL my supporters and followers. Thank you for being the wonderful courageous souls that you are.

I want to give a special heartfelt 'thank you' to my God-fearing best friend for being my biggest supporter. Mr. BJ Canty, of Thomasville, North Carolina. Thank you for being YOU! Much love to you always…

Preface

In this book, "Embrace Your Shadow" I am presenting various parts of ourselves that determine who we are as a person. In fact, many factors contribute to who someone is, such as genetics, environment, and life experiences. I will primarily be focusing on personality traits, self-respect, self-esteem, listening and communication, listening to understand, and what necessary changes you could put in effect to improve your life for the better. Also, I will list some ways you can turn some of those stumbling blocks into stepping stones.

Acts 15:12-21 of the Bible states, "We help others grow when we turn stumbling blocks into stepping stones." Therefore, with the information we discuss, you will be able to learn how to not only improve the areas of your life, but you will grasp the realization of how important it is to protect your personal space.

God is trying to prepare you so you can move into YOUR destiny….Yes, YOUR destiny is YOURS…RUN TOWARD IT!!!

Table of Contents

Introduction

Ladies and Gentlemen, in this book, "Embrace Your Shadow" I will be elaborating on what makes us who we are and what parts of us could always use improvement. The objective here is to recognize our downfalls and put in the work to turn our weaknesses into strengths. In doing so, we can strive for more positive results in our relationships. Before you can put the work into your relationships you have to see what areas you need to become more serious about. The differences in personalities, attitudes, and character of an individual will often dictate how they react to the adversities in life.

Adversities are defined as misfortune, hardship, or a troubling situation that can affect people throughout their lives. Some types of adversities that you may encounter or have encountered in life include physical injury or illness, self-doubt, rejection, poverty, losing a loved one, or even career struggles. The proper strategies on how to face adversities head-on consist of staying disciplined, refraining from making excuses, maintaining a positive attitude, caring for yourself, and no matter what you do, never giving up.

If you want to live a peaceful life filled with faith, respect, and understanding, there are certain traits in us that we should be firm on, especially when it comes to boundaries. How we feel about ourselves reveals how we allow others to treat us, as well as how we live our lives. I will make it clear that I judge no one and do not have the authority to do so. However, within my personal journey and having confronted many different obstacles, I am inspired to help others in areas where with a few major changes, your whole life can take a drastic turn for the better.

As we grow and as we are presented with certain situations in life's journey it is critical to know that your character, your self-esteem, your self-respect, your communication skills, and most importantly, your listening skills determine not only what we face, but how we respond to what obstacles we encounter in life. "Embrace Your Shadow" explains how each part is important, what steps you can take to ensure better approaches and solutions and shows you how to eliminate any personal boundaries that you might encounter.

Upon reading this book, you will have better knowledge of who you are and why you have experienced so many issues within your life and relationships. With the information you gather here, you will be able to make the necessary changes within yourself and your environment; so those moments of pain can result in how to live peacefully and happily, regardless of what you have been through.

Chapter 1

Self-Respect &
Self-Esteem

As we begin, the first and most important question is, "Who are you?" From your characteristics to your personality, all the way down to beliefs, morals, and values. Have you ever found yourself in deep thought about yourself and all you have been through? Our character is revealed through how we treat others. It is only right that you treat others in the manner that you desire to be treated, which is disclosed by the way you respect, love, protect, and care for yourself every single day.

The scripture in Proverbs 4:23 clearly states, "Above all else, guard your heart, for everything you do flows from it." If you think about this, we do not guard anything that has no value, but in any case, remember that your heart is extremely valuable. You are probably asking, "How do I ask God to guard my heart?" Pray this prayer:

> *"Father God, today I put on the Armor of God. I strap on the belt of truth of your Word. I thank You that You are good, that You are faithful, that You are my defender, and You protect me. Please guard and protect my heart from the enemy. In Jesus' name, I pray. Amen."*

Have you ever heard the saying, "It doesn't matter how beautiful you are on the outside, if your attitude is ugly then you are just ugly?" No one wants to be in the presence of someone who depletes them of their energy and exhausts them of their peace. The process of evaluation, as discussed in my first book, "Dazzling Scars, a Self-Help Book" provides questions to my readers that allow them to evaluate themselves and determine why they continue to experience the same issues during their lives. So, knowing who you are at this point in your life, your self-respect, what you allow and what you don't allow, and what type of attitude and character you display will assist in why you have a content life or why it seems like you are always in some kind of drama.

Starting a list is a wonderful way to come up with solutions to any issues you face. Section your paper into two columns. At the top of column one, write what you love about yourself. At the top of column two, list what you dislike about yourself. Therefore, the answers you come up with are telling you if they will work toward your future or if they will paralyze it.

Now that you have made your list of what you love and dislike about yourself, ask yourself what you need to do to ensure the necessary changes in your life. By using your list and being truthful to yourself you will need to understand that these changes will have to consist of consistency, discipline, and focus to result in a positive change.

Although God has His perfect plan designed for us, it is only necessary that we do our part in upholding the faith, which is ensuring and trusting that He has our best interest at heart.

Keep in mind that God will NOT bless mess. According to Romans 8:28, "And we know that in all things God works for the good of those who love Him, who have been called according to His purpose." So, studying your self-love list, I ask you the question, "Who are you?"

At this point in your life are you able to say that your level of self-respect is firm in knowing your worth? Do you set solid boundaries within your relationships? Or do you compromise your boundaries depending on how you feel about someone? Do you have issues standing up for yourself? Do you like to keep feelings to yourself to "Keep the Peace?"

Self-respect comes with respecting your mind, body, emotions, and your soul. Building self-respect means that you are staying true to your values and not compromising them. The more you stand on this the more you will feel fulfilled and confident in who you are. Being kind to yourself is one way to promote self-respect. In addition, ask yourself, *what makes you happy*? Do not compare yourself to others and always manifest positivity about yourself. Always be sure that you treat yourself exceptionally well so you realize how others should treat you.

Along with self-respect comes self-esteem. Where would you say you are in this area? There are three levels of self-esteem, and they include: low, healthy, and excessive. Keep in mind that self-esteem may change with age; how a person was raised and their behavior throughout life that molded them can also affect their self-esteem.

So, low self-esteem is feeling inferior, "less than others." Healthy self-esteem is having an accurate and balanced self-view of self. For example, respecting yourself is the first step toward understanding that you are deserving of love, consideration, and opportunities like everyone else. With excessive, overly high self-esteem, you display the traits that you feel superior to others. In most cases, those who possess excessive self-esteem are often arrogant, self-indulgent, and express feelings of entitlement. As you meet people in life you will be able to determine this as the conversation flows.

A quote that stood out to me by Agnes Karee Schwest Krankenpflesa stated, "A healthy person has a thousand wishes. A sick person only has one." This quote speaks volumes. In honoring your emotions, you are allowing yourself to feel whatever you are feeling. Suppressing or ignoring them is self-destructive and it keeps the root cause intact and prevents you from growing. When you are analyzing where these emotions came from, think about how you treat others because what a person tends to dislike in others is usually a reflection of what we dislike in ourselves.

Keep in mind that these feelings contribute to the self-respect and self-esteem you possess within your own being. From elaborating on self-respect, do you feel you respect yourself? Always, sometimes, or rarely? Would you say you have low, healthy, or excessive self-esteem? Stress and difficult life events can have a negative effect on self-esteem.

Many factors play a role in how we feel about ourselves. These factors include:

1- Social Media

2- Difficult early life experiences

3- Mental health conditions such as anxiety and depression

4- Beliefs can contribute to your sense of self-worth.

5- Friends and family

6- Work environment

7- Physical/Emotional abuse is a major risk factor associated with low self-esteem.

Understand that your self-esteem and respect for yourself can be improved through strategies that can assist in fixing low self-esteem. Try these strategies:

1- Use hopeful statements meaning be kind and encouraging to yourself.

2- Forgive yourself; everyone makes mistakes.

3- Focus on what is positive.

4- Try new approaches.

5- Encourage yourself with daily affirmations and positive compliments.

6- Redirect negative thoughts to the "bright side."

The strategies can be helpful to you with the motivation and discipline you set forth for yourself. The first thing you need to be sure of is that you are not comparing yourself to other people. God created a unique divine individual in you. Find that beauty inside of yourself and let it shine. Letting negative people go and setting boundaries in your relationships will help surround you with more positive and solid people. You have a say-so on how you would like your life to flow. In fact, recognizing your levels of self-respect and self-esteem will determine what trials you encounter in life. Make a firm decision to be better and STAND ON IT!!

Chapter 2

Listen Carefully;
Observe Closely

Have you ever had a conversation with someone and felt as though you have known them for years? The connection feels so good that you both exchange numbers. As days go by you both talk and text each other daily, feeling as though this person is *too good to be true*. At this point, you are on cloud nine wondering where this person has been your whole life. What you're feeling is very fulfilling, but it is also a sign that we need to slow down because timing is everything.

As you focus on being an amazing attentive listener just remember that there is far more to listening than hearing. An attentive listener not only listens to what is being said, but they also pay close attention to what is left unsaid or partially said. Effective listening involves observation of body language as well as noticing any inconsistencies between verbal and nonverbal messages.

Below are a few principles behind exceptional listening:

1- Stop talking; Listen to others without interrupting or talking over their thoughts.

2- Prepare yourself to listen; be attentive to your speaker and concentrate on the message they are communicating.

3- Remove distractions.

4- Emphasize; try to understand the speakers' point of view.

5- Listen to the tone; it is not what a person says, but how they say it.

6- Observe any non-verbal communication, including body language, gestures, facial expressions, and eye movements.

Using a few of these will improve listening skills, but by observing actions, your speakers' message will be quite clear.

In James 1:19-20 the Bible clearly states, "Know this, my beloved brothers: let every person be quick to hear, slow to speak, slow to anger; for the anger of man does not produce the righteousness of God." Now you should know how listening and observing are vital to any form of relationship that you have with others. For example, if someone you are communicating with says they are not upset about you noticing a crease in their forehead then it clearly shows they could be. Actions speak much louder than words. It is wise to know that you always need to be cautious in what a person tells you, but always trust what they show you.

As for observing closely, the benefit of doing so enables you to identify patterns in a person's behavior. As you pay close attention you will be able to notice small details of a person that could be particularly important or relevant to you in case you would like to pursue the moment. Also, being attentive to body language and facial expressions can help us better understand the feelings and experiences of others, which leads to a greater sense of empathy and understanding.

So, now that we have discussed how listening and observing come hand in hand, how would you describe your listening and observation skills? Do you focus on words more than actions, or vice versa? You can uncover more than you realize by paying close attention to the person you interact with. In doing so, you're able to visualize the red flags that you can avoid; or if you continue to interact with that person, it will be the red flags you pay for down the road. Pay Attention!

Chapter 3

Communication Styles & Skills

The biggest communication problem is that we, as people, don't listen to understand, we listen to respond. Even though there may be times when you feel as though you have a lot to say, sometimes it is best to say nothing at all. In fact, reacting will only result in dealing with the same problems over and over without achieving any solution or eliminating the issue. When you allow someone to speak while you remain silent, it shows them both respect and appreciation. Having respect for someone as they speak can bring forth stronger relationships. This will show your speaker that you care about what they have to say.

You may be asking yourself, *why is communication a topic in this book?* Well, whether we choose to believe it or not, communication is vital to any relationship you engage in. The word choices and tone of your speaker can reveal their emotions, especially if they are quick to respond and do it with anger.

There are several communication styles that we use every day. Gaining knowledge of each one and what it includes will also help you determine what type of individual you have encountered. Also, knowing the styles of communication will help you learn how to respond effectively.

Below are some communication styles, along with their meanings, so you can recognize them in others.

1- Aggressive- this style involves dominating the conversation by asking questions rudely and issuing commands while failing to listen to others.

2- Passive- avoiding the opportunity to express your opinions or feelings, while protecting the needs of others.

3- Assertive- communicating in a confident, firm, and professional manner, while allowing others to express their opinions.

4- Manipulative- communicating in such a way that attempts to control the person or the situation. The manipulators may already have schemes or plans in their minds, and they may influence people through their words.

5- Affiliative- collaborative style of interaction that involves positive information and sharing power and responsibilities amongst each other while also being empathetic towards others.

6- Expressive- outgoing communication where a person can communicate or write their wants, needs, feelings, and thoughts.

7- Submissive- pleasing others to avoid conflict.

By having knowledge of these examples, you can determine who you communicate with, whether it be at home, work, school, or any public setting. It is important to identify someone's communication style so it can help you develop and deliver your message clearly, thus enabling you to prevent conflicts and build successful relationships.

Using this information can give you a clearer insight into how to respond or react to certain character traits within your relationships. Although all relationships experience ups and downs, no one, under any circumstance, deserves to be treated unfairly or in an unhealthy manner. If you are experiencing any of these behaviors or issues with communication, try to re-evaluate yourself and your situation.

If you have not yet purchased my first book, "Dazzling Scars" you may like to because it is a self-help book where you learn how to evaluate yourself to determine what personal traits you acquire that allow an attraction between yourself and toxic people. Keep in mind that silence can be so powerful, especially upon meeting someone new and learning who they are.

Don't be in a rush, JUST LISTEN!!

Chapter 4

Rejection is Protection

I believe that most people agree with situations in relationships because they fear disagreements, which could lead to rejection. One thing I have learned over the years with relationships is that God is going to reveal what needs to be seen without you having to lift a finger. We all have the desire to be loved, but we fail to realize that does not include tolerating unnecessary toxic behaviors from others. The way we present ourselves to others will portray to them what we will allow. So, once they see that you are a tolerator you may as well be prepared to face some disrespect and nonsense because people will do things to see how far they can go with you. The more you allow and the more you address it, the worse it gets.

Moreover, creating healthy firm boundaries will only reveal who is for you and who is not. We all have met someone and became attracted to them and desired more than a friendship but got heartbroken because the other person did not desire one. The rejection can be quite hurtful. I have personally experienced rejection a couple of times in my life, and it was heartbreaking, so I can relate to the hurt that comes from it. When people say they choose to be alone, in most cases, it is because they fear being rejected or heartbroken. When we invest so much into a relationship and then find out that they never cared about us as we thought, it really destroys a person. In fact, we saw the signs as they interacted with us, but we hoped the love that we showered them with would show them we were worth more than the manner in which they treated us. We often may find ourselves trying to prove that we are worthy when we will never have to do that with the person who is meant for us. Your value will always go unnoticed by a person who is not tied to your destiny.

As you continue with life and feel as though you are constantly rejected, remember, that although it hurts, God knows what you deserve and will not allow you to settle for less. If you feel you are never at peace with a person, God is trying to protect you from any harm that may be on course. This could be a hard truth to accept, especially when you already fell head over heels for this person. This is when we turn to God first and reflect on who he is. Jesus endured pain and rejection for our sake, so if our Savior of the world can hold rejection in one hand and love for us in the other, then we can endure the pain that is caused by rejection.

When we don't understand why we have been rejected, we can learn to view rejection through Him. Through His Word, He teaches us that we're able to handle rejection in a way that can bring healing to the areas of our lives that acquire the most hurt.

So, when you feel you are being rejected by someone, remember that God is in control, and He sees better for you. A special person in my life always told me, "Don't always receive a message in a negative way; try finding the bright side in it." Now I understand exactly what he meant by this.

However, understand that the root cause of rejection could have emerged from painful childhood experiences. The causes could be coming from being excluded by one's peers, or from the painful feeling of being unloved by your parents or other family members. In addition, other triggers could include traumatic experiences of rejection or even abandonment. Therefore, coming to terms with the underlying cause of why a person fears rejection could help with healing in this area.

Most importantly, I can emphasize that rejection should be used to your advantage as a sign that improvement is needed instead of a way to become depressed or dispirited. Learning who you are and who you portray yourself to be to others will give you a more valid definition of why the fear of rejection is so common, yet so satisfying, knowing that God loves us so much that He refuses to allow us to settle for anything. Everything we encounter and face is a part of the journey to our destiny. Cherish every moment!

Chapter 5

Stepping Stones

After discussing who you are and topics of self-respect, self-esteem, and communication styles, you will be able to determine your strengths and weaknesses. There are always areas of improvement in all our lives. No matter what you have endured over the years, it's never too late for you to use all of your experiences as stepping stones. The stepping stones you create will be included among your achievements and successes. For those who said you would never amount to anything, there's one stone.

Anytime someone treats you in a way you do not deserve, it is another stone added to your success. Use all of the negative situations that arise as stepping stones to create a beautiful successful life for yourself. It is never too late. Remember, it is not what anyone says about you, it is what God says about you. That is the only opinion that matters. On Judgment Day, you will face no one other than God so be sure you are living to please Him and no one else. You are His divine creation.

Difficult circumstances will come into our lives, but as we grow, our intellectual capacity will increase. Therefore, it is important to know that challenges aren't meant to be stumbling blocks; instead, they are meant to serve as stepping stones that will make our lives better by leading us back to God. He is the only one who can change your situation. All you need to do is surrender your life to Him. How long are you going to sit around and feel worthless and feel sorry for yourself? You are an intelligent unique creation that God made you to be. The talents that He has blessed you with are to be used to serve others. Look deep inside yourself and find what you do well. The gift He blessed you with, He blessed you with for a purpose. You can do anything that you set your mind to.

Don't allow your gift to go to waste. Use it and use it passionately and start creating the life that God intended for you. You are worth so much more than that for which you settle. God made you to stand out, not to follow a soul. He just wants you to trust Him and have Faith to know if you do what you need to do, He will handle the rest. Life is beautiful when you start looking toward a better life and make the effort toward a life worth living. No one deserves to be hindered by anyone out of jealousy, envy, or because they lack the ambition to strive for success themselves.

28

Chapter 6

Make Necessary Changes

By now, you should have recognized some areas within you, which can use some improvement. You're probably wondering how you can even begin to make the necessary changes. Well, recognition is #1 and you have already done that so now with evaluation comes the solution.

Many resources are available to assist you with some of the issues you may have. There are support groups available, as well as online channels that give great advice on the specific areas you need to work on. Also, there are coaches/mentors available who have specialized in helping us work through different areas of our lives to assist us in becoming who God designed us to be.

The process is never easy, but one thing I can guarantee you is it's worth it! Let go of all that weight that is not yours to carry and start with what makes you happy and what makes you feel good about yourself. It is work but the results are amazing and remember… you are not alone.

God says in Deuteronomy 31:8, "The Lord Himself goes before you and will be with you; He will never leave you nor forsake you. Do not be afraid; do not be discouraged." To an advantage, learning who you are, why you are the way you are, and why you think the way you do will reveal the answers to how many undeserving obstacles came forth in your life in the first place. While making the necessary changes, you can follow the 3 R's. The 3 R's are Recognize, Re-evaluate, and Retry. We are human. We all make mistakes, but we also learn through the struggles that lessons are meant to be learned from, not repeated. Identifying parts of yourself that need healing and work will only help YOU! The courageous person God built inside you is on the path He designed for you. YOU CAN do this!

Chapter 7

Protect Your Space

I will be the one to inform you that during your growth process, some people from your circle will fall off. God will reveal the hearts of those around you. For example, in my past relationship with a narcissist, I noticed that all he cared about was making money and owning a business but never wanted to do the actual work. My blessings were delayed because of the people I was connected to. God put me in a position that hurt my heart because He knew that unless I was hurt to that extreme, I would never leave. I am an empath, and I am not a quitter.

So, God knows my heart and He knew if He blessed me I would share it with the one person that I "thought" cared about me. I knew by the disrespect and the accusations that my ex didn't care whether I came or left, but one thing I did know is that all those accusations were confessions of what he was doing. There were many nights I would pray that God would give me the strength to just let go and not look back.

Narcissists are self-centered individuals who require attention and validation from anyone who makes them feel important. They lie, accuse, disrespect, blame, gaslight, and abuse their partner mentally, physically, emotionally, and financially. They expect loyalty and explanations from you that they cannot and will not reciprocate. They feel they have some type of control over you. To receive the blessings that God has for you, you will need to remove yourself from the ones that are not a part of your destiny.

The hurtful part is it is hard to accept that the ones we thought loved us so much didn't and instead, they have been using and abusing our love and goodness the entire time. Always keep in mind that God has a time for everything, and you must trust that for yourself and your life. Protecting your space includes using the discernment God blessed you with to use your gift and determine what kind of person you are involved with. Discernment is defined as the ability to make a smart judgment about something; a wise way of judging between things or a particular way of seeing things.

You have the authority to remove anyone in your circle or life that is interfering with your boundaries or peace. There should be no room for negotiation. When you stand firm on your boundaries you are respecting yourself, and showing others what you will or will not tolerate.

There is nothing comparable to peace. Having acquired that peace is the best feeling ever, especially when you align yourself with respect and take control of what makes YOU happy. As you protect your space and who you allow in your life, you will be able to recognize who is meant for your journey and who is not.

Those who respect you will respect the decisions you have set forth for bettering yourself. When you get confused just stop and think about the saying, *"What is good to you is not always good for you."* What is for YOU is for YOU- In God's Time!

34

Chapter 8

God's Divine Timing

I am more than sure we all can relate to the topic of impatience. Impatience is defined as not wanting to wait for things. When we feel so good about something and we begin to think with our emotions, rather than logically, we tend to become frustrated. I have been that person for years and it becomes stressful. I am in a season now where I am learning to wait on God. He has a time and place for everything. It took some struggles in my life to make me realize that what I want right away always has a consequence. So, impatience has its roots in frustration. Every single time we feel that our wants and wishes are being ignored by God, we start to stress.

Just because we feel so strongly about something does not mean it is meant to be. God made us to rely on Him and not on our own understanding. The benefit of things that are immediately accessible makes us not only think we have to have it, but that we have to have it NOW! It is important to recognize when impatience is involved, that those moments are not aligned with God's timing. At that moment, we should pray to God about what we would like but also know that if it is meant for us to have it then we will.

In James 1:3 it states, "Patience is developed through tests and trials and through the practice of walking with the spirit. To a disadvantage, impatience can put a strain on relationships within your life. Being impatient or easily agitated can cause conflicts with the people around you and could result in damaging those relationships. In Ephesians 4:2 it states, "Be completely humble and be gentle; be patient, bearing with one another in love."

It is important to recognize where your impatience has been rooted. High-stress levels can cause us to be impatient, but also the lack of control over a situation can cause us to be more impatient. If you happen to be a person who is easily annoyed or provoked, then your impatience shows. If you are having trouble with being patient, pray for patience and pray for the Lord to give it to you. No matter what you do, do not stop there. You must pray for Him to teach it, grow it, and most importantly help you understand how crucial it is to practice patience when times become difficult.

The most common time we become impatient is when situations seem challenging or uncomfortable. Always take heed that God helps us grow through the challenges. However, as an individual who personally struggles with impatience at times, it is essential that in order to grow in patience, the first step is accepting discomfort. Also, being mindful and a good listener helps improve impatience. We can make a conscious effort to manage our negative emotions, reframe challenging situations and keep our focus on our goals.

Jesus' patience resided in the fact that He was doing His Father's perfect will and redeeming His people. Therefore, Jesus was patient with His people, His enemies, and His Father. See, if the fruit of the spirit is to make us more Christ-like, then we can see how Jesus displayed perfect endurance without EVER complaining.

With all the information that has been stated, it is extremely crucial in our lives that we remain patient and understand that everything that is destined to happen for us only happens, in God's Divine Timing, and not what we want when we want it. Ecclesiastes 3:1 tells us that God is a God of timing: "There is an appointed time for everything. And there is a time for every event under heaven."

As stated in A1 Overview, God's divine timing is the idea that everything happens exactly when it is supposed to, and that God orchestrates ALL events not only to help us grow but also to evolve. It is not about our own desires or timeline, but rather it's about God's Will and Plan. The Power of God's Divine Timing gives us the ability to bring forth peace, clarity, and a deep sense of purpose.

By understanding God's Divine Timing, we can gain many benefits in our lives. The benefits include:

1- Reduced stress and anxiety

2- Increased self-awareness

3- Greater sense of purpose

Trusting the timing God has for our lives helps us have a better understanding of our life's purpose.

The Bible says that we must trust that everything in our lives has an appointed time. It's only for our good. While you wait for God to instruct you to move, you can continue to spend time with Him regularly, continue serving Him, maintain hope, recognize the lessons He gives you, and always reflect on the Goodness of God in your personal life. In realization, seasons of waiting can become tough when you feel that God is not hearing your prayers. Trust God, focus on the positive, and remind yourself of Romans 12:2 where God encourages His children to renew their minds.

There are many reasons God makes us wait. First and foremost, He wants us to become closer to Him. He wants us to know that we need no one but Him, in EVERY season. As stated in Hebrews 13:5, "I will never leave you nor forsake you." As for relationships, God's timing is extremely important.

Nowadays, we rush into relationships only to rush out. The reason behind that is we like some things about someone, and then we start thinking we will automatically love this person and live happily ever after. I really wish it were that easy, but God never makes it that simple. He gives us a mind, intuition, and discernment to be able to see something for what it is. In fact, we are the ones who ignore certain signs and red flags because we "like" someone. With all the resources God gives us to apply in our lives, we always think our way is better. Let me say that when we make our plans, I honestly believe that God laughs at us. He sits back saying things like, "Oh really? Let me show you my child why you may want this but it's not what you need to fulfill my Plan."

Therefore, you need to trust that God is in complete control and just sit back and enjoy the ride of life. As for my personal life, I have always rushed into relationships without taking the time to get knowledge of how someone thinks, acts, and handles situations on a day-to-day basis. So, for not establishing a strong solid foundation as friends first, the whole relationship failed. As I am older now, I realize how valuable time is, although I still have moments where I find myself becoming impatient.

I am only God's servant and will be until the day He takes me home. I will forever learn new things every new day and I accept that as an individual. God is my Protector and the *Boss,* so I trust Him with all I have and with all the lessons He brings forth in my life. There is a reason behind every morning we wake up, a reason that we endure so many challenges, and a reason that God puts us in a position to cross paths with certain people. Trusting God, His Purpose for your life, and His Plan will push you closer to the destiny that He has for you.

As Bishop Dale Bronner states, "Time is a great healer, concealer, revealer, and a secret weapon that forces deception to reveal itself."

42

Chapter 9

Embrace Your Shadow

As you sit and reflect on every moment you have experienced in your life, remember that God designs everything to happen for a reason. That reason is to fulfill the purpose He planned for your life. Upon accepting who you once were and who you have grown to be, you will be able to learn the lessons behind the situations He has put you in. Within your growth process, you will be able to see the lessons behind the situations you have endured. You will be able to see what has happened and why He put you in the situations you experienced, to begin with.

As you enter a storm you will always have questions, but remember it is best not to question what God is doing, it is best to trust the process and come to realize there is a lesson behind the storm. You will never be the same person after the storm as you were when you entered it.

To grow you will need to accept who you are and surrender your all to God and He will take it from there. A lot of times we postpone our blessings by being connected to the wrong people. Personally, in my life, I have endured so many hardships only because I chose to try and lean on my own understanding, like God wasn't going to *check me...* and He did just that!

At times we do not realize that God is putting us on a path to teach us a lesson and until we learn the lesson we will continue to repeat the same situation, just in different people. We *think* we can make our OWN plans but consequently, it doesn't work that way.

I am not the same person I was a year ago, not even four months ago. God has done so much work in me within the last year and had me in isolation so that I could come to terms with the decisions I made in my life. It was emotional to have to accept the fact that I was responsible for everything I participated in, and when I say that forgiving myself was hard, but it saved my life.

Once I forgave myself and began giving more and more of my time to God, I noticed that my life began to take a turn for the better. It's like my whole life was renewed, to where the people I was once attracted to didn't fascinate me anymore. To be honest, I have found myself quite disgusted by the mess I tolerated in the past.

Even though God did the best work in me through my process, He is still expanding my vision of Him. The relationship that I have with Him is closer than I have ever had. I rely on Him for everything in my life. I know that there is no way that I can ever go wrong with Him being the *Head* of my life.

There are many storms that we will face in our lives but one thing to remember is that our decisions will always affect our destiny. God wants us to have a Spiritual Mind. Romans 8:6 states that God wants you to have a mind focused on your spirit. The Scripture warns us not to make our minds into our masters. We are instructed to train our thoughts and turn our thoughts over to God. The most important thing that God asks of us is to love the Lord. In His plan we are given lessons to learn from that will help us reach our destiny.

Therefore, here are some steps that may help you fulfill your destiny:

1- Define your goals.

2- Plan for obstacles because they will arise.

3- Use the talents or spiritual gifts God blessed you with.

4- Challenge yourself because challenges stimulate growth.

5- People and experiences can reveal truths about yourself.

6- Always surround yourself with positive people.

7- Be productive.

8- Always respond in the spirit and NOT in the flesh

9- Understand that destiny demands that you remain focused.

10- DO NOT allow disappointments or discouragement to make you want to quit.

Furthermore, it is best to start your day off with prayer so that you let God know you have Him in your life as a priority, as well as the Faith that you trust Him with all that you face. Prayer life is essential for everyone who carries God as their personal Savior.

During your reading of this book, all the traits you recognized about yourself can be transformed with God's help. Now is your time to put the work in and allow God to do the rest. My people, love all the qualities that made you who you are. It's never too late for improvement. Tomorrow is NOT promised, so, start TODAY! Allow God to work in your life.

You are not your mistakes or your scars, so I'll say it again, *Embrace Your Shadow!!!*

48

Conclusion

In concluding this book, I have specified the various parts of ourselves, including our character and personality traits that make us who we are. The purpose of presenting this information was so that you can evaluate where you are in each of the subjects and determine what in your life has been hindering you from living the life that God has intended for you.

A change in your life cannot occur until YOU make the recognition. Therefore, with recognition comes a solution. Consequently, we will come through stumbling blocks during our journey, but God said He will never leave us nor forsake us. With the stumbling blocks comes the advantage of using them to create stepping stones to build a more positive abundant life that God intends for you. In doing so, the work seems difficult, but trust me when I say it is soooooooo worth it!

Make the changes necessary so that you can begin living the life that was designed for you. Remember, YOUR destiny was designed for no one else, but YOU. Embrace your shadow and all the situations that built you into who you are today. You may say it was a difficult journey, but that journey will forever be worth the results that you are now living. Speak positivity into your life because the words you speak will manifest over your life. Embrace your path to your destiny and RUN TOWARD IT!!!

About the Author

udrey Adams was born and raised in Cicero, which is a suburb outside the city of Chicago, Illinois. She currently resides in Valdosta, Georgia, near her immediate family.

Audrey is a Daughter, Mother, and Grandmother who loves God, and her family, as well as writing, traveling, and helping others become the best version of themselves.

Due to a few unhealthy/abusive relationships in the past, Audrey has not only used her knowledge to apply in her personal life, but she has been given an assignment from God to assist those who need the power and motivation to break through abusive relationships.

In July of 2023, Audrey joined the YouTube channel created by Hario Ovadtop, which focuses on narcissistic relationships, and remains a dedicated member of his channel. She has gained knowledge through her personal experience with dating a narcissist and has also researched more behaviors on how to detect an individual who displays toxic traits.

To an advantage, Audrey has become the voice that some may be fearful to use. She desires to help many people throughout the world by using certain strategies and evaluating what personal traits they need to improve so they can work toward healthier relationships with others. "The desire for help begins with self."

Embrace Your Shadow is Audrey Adams' second published book. Her first published book was ***Dazzling Scars***.

www.ingramcontent.com/pod-product-compliance
Lightning Source LLC
Chambersburg PA
CBHW050613160726
48003CB00003B/1172